SUPER CUTE!

Baby Pigs

by Christina Leaf

BELLWETHER MEDIA • MINNEAPOLIS, MN

Note to Librarians, Teachers, and Parents:

Blastoff! Readers are carefully developed by literacy experts and combine standards-based content with developmentally appropriate text.

Level 1 provides the most support through repetition of high-frequency words, light text, predictable sentence patterns, and strong visual support.

Level 2 offers early readers a bit more challenge through varied simple sentences, increased text load, and less repetition of high-frequency words.

Level 3 advances early-fluent readers toward fluency through increased text and concept load, less reliance on visuals, longer sentences, and more literary language.

Level 4 builds reading stamina by providing more text per page, increased use of punctuation, greater variation in sentence patterns, and increasingly challenging vocabulary.

Level 5 encourages children to move from "learning to read" to "reading to learn" by providing even more text, varied writing styles, and less familiar topics.

Whichever book is right for your reader, Blastoff! Readers are the perfect books to build confidence and encourage a love of reading that will last a lifetime!

This edition first published in 2014 by Bellwether Media, Inc.

No part of this publication may be reproduced in whole or in part without written permission of the publisher. For information regarding permission, write to Bellwether Media, Inc., Attention: Permissions Department, 5357 Penn Avenue South, Minneapolis, MN 55419.

Library of Congress Cataloging-in-Publication Data

Leaf, Christina, author.
  Baby Pigs / by Christina Leaf.
    pages cm. – (Blastoff! Readers. Super Cute!)
  Summary: "Developed by literacy experts for students in kindergarten through grade three, this book introduces baby pigs to young readers through leveled text and related photos"– Provided by publisher.
  Audience: Ages 5-8.
  Audience: K to grade 3.
  Includes bibliographical references and index.
  ISBN 978-1-60014-975-7 (hardcover : alk. paper)
  1. Piglets–Juvenile literature. 2. Animals–Infancy–Juvenile literature. I. Title.
  SF395.5.L43 2014
  636.4'07–dc23
                              2013050259

Printed in the United States of America, North Mankato, MN.

Table of Contents

Piglets!

Baby pigs are called piglets. They live on farms.

Life With the Litter

Piglets are born in **litters**. Each litter has 9 to 15 babies.

Newborn piglets **huddle** together. They sleep in a pile to keep warm.

Piglets drink mom's milk together. Each has its own spot to **nurse**.

Older piglets eat **grains** from a **trough**. The farmer feeds them.

Piglets also **root** for food in the dirt. They dig with their **snouts**.

Playful Piglets

Piglets love to play. Brothers and sisters chase one another.

Sometimes they play with piglets from other litters.

Then the piglets
roll in the mud
to cool off.
What fun!

Glossary

grains—the small, hard seeds of plants such as wheat, corn, and rice

huddle—to gather close together

litters—groups of babies that are born together

newborn—just born

nurse—to drink mom's milk

root—to dig in the ground

snouts—the noses of pigs

trough—a long, shallow container for an animal's food

To Learn More

AT THE LIBRARY

Falconer, Ian. *Olivia*. New York, N.Y.: Atheneum Books for Young Readers, 2000.

Kalman, Bobbie. *Baby Pigs*. New York, N.Y.: Crabtree, 2010.

Older, Jules. *Pig*. Watertown, Mass.: Charlesbridge, 2004.

ON THE WEB

Learning more about pigs is as easy as 1, 2, 3.

1. Go to www.factsurfer.com.

2. Enter "pigs" into the search box.

3. Click the "Surf" button and you will see a list of related web sites.

With factsurfer.com, finding more information is just a click away.

Index

The images in this book are reproduced through the courtesy of: S-F, front cover; Klein-Hubert/ Kimballstock, pp. 4-5, 8-9; Jan Mastnik, pp. 6-7; Tsekhmister, pp. 10-11; Grant Heilman Photography/ Alamy, pp. 12-13; J.L. Klein & M.L. Hubert/ Biosphoto, pp. 14-15; Juniors/ SuperStock, pp. 16-17; Biosphoto/ SuperStock, pp. 18-19; talseN, pp. 20-21.